Ireland Revisited

IRELAND

JILL URIS

DOUBLEDAY & COMPANY, INC., GARDEN CITY, NEW YORK

REVISITED

By Jill Uris

IRELAND *A TERRIBLE BEAUTY*
JERUSALEM *SONG OF SONGS*
IRELAND REVISITED

IRELAND REVISITED

with words of the following Irish writers and Irishmen: (in order of appearance)

George Moore
C. E. Montague
James Joyce
W. B. Yeats
Seumas MacManus
W. R. Rodgers
George Bernard Shaw
Des Lavelle
Marshall Hutson
Pátraic Ó Conaire
Brian Friel
Sean O'Casey
Bryan MacMahon
John Betjeman
Fanny Parnell

Lady Gregory
J. M. Synge
Robert Emmet
Padraic Pearse
Mary Lavin
Winifred M. Letts
Les Casey
Dennis Smith
Tomas O Crohan
Peig Sayers
Roger Casement

and the following writers of Ireland:

Leon Uris
Eugene O'Neill

DESIGNED BY LAURENCE ALEXANDER

ISBN: 0-385-17616-3
Library of Congress Catalog Card Number: 81-43402
Copyright © 1982 by Jill Uris

Uris, Jill, 1947-
    Ireland revisited.

    1. Ireland—Description and travel—1951-
—Views. 2. Northern Ireland—Description and travel—Views. I. Title.
DA982.U74   914.1504824   81-43402   AACR2

For Lee, my favorite "Irish writer"

I wish to acknowledge the assistance and gracious hospitality of my dear Irish friends, Ray and Kevin Diffley, whose contribution enhanced this volume greatly.

Contents

Waiting for the Creamery Van, County Kerry

The Mystical Call of Ireland

Ireland's greatest heroes are neither fighters nor politicians but saints and scholars. Her backbone is her legends and her literature. From the sixth century on Ireland was the light of the Western world which wallowed in the Dark Ages. Irish monastic settlements became great learning centers for Christians throughout Europe and her missionaries are credited with initiating and salvaging the religion on a darkened continent. Magnificent illuminated manuscripts from the era are among the world's great treasures of the past.

Legends are like comets in the fanciful Irish mind and every town has its share of mythical and historic tales and its bards who recite the ballads of heritage to this day. Literature, like nothing else, is synonymous with Irish culture. The list of fine poets, playwrights and storytellers is endless, whereas one is hard pressed to recall more than a few outstanding painters or musicians. Words form personalities and language became her battle legions for the perennially impoverished Irish had few weapons with which to fight the Britannic power which overran her.

In Ireland both the literature and the landscape tell the story of centuries of tragedy. Death once stalked the land and reminders can still be seen in the form of bones of abandoned houses, memorials to the great potato famine of the 1840s and other disasters. Homes inhabited for generations were destroyed by the battering ram to clear the land for cattle grazing or abandoned by those forced to emigrate. Once lively, flourishing communities never recovered from the loss of their sons and daughters and of life itself. Peasants everywhere cling to the land, but in Ireland, the obsession for land has resulted in a love-hate relationship. They longed for what had been taken from them by the "strangers" while at the same time they were fearful of the land that had failed them.

The Irish writers show little romanticism for the land. What they have produced is a literature of remembrance overwhelmingly shaded with death and dying, wakes, cemeteries and graves. They write not for prophecy but for memory and especially the memory of family and the little things of daily life. American literature echoes grandeur, heroism, wealth and power and great social issues, whereas in Irish literature the painting of a cupboard or a walk into town from the fields can be as grand a happening as an army at war or the crossing of the prairies.

Mysticism and fantasy pervade the literature as a quest for life beyond suffering and life beyond death. Like those fickle mists which hover then tease with only a moment's glimpse of a magnificent view, mysticism, fantasy and an illusory religion give brief hope and escape from the harsh realities. But with all the spiritualism the saving grace of the Irish is their mastery of laughing at themselves, producing a constant chuckle which only adds to that elusive charm. They speak, not as men and women talking, but as fencing masters.

After Leon and I finished our previous Irish books we returned on an odyssey to find the fictional locations of Trinity. The towns, churches, pubs and characters were all there as were many adventures.

Leaving behind the outside world we traveled the River Shannon from one end to the other in a houseboat. What a wonderful escape! However, we did have a problem of two captains and no crew or two crew and no captain. The resulting "discussions" (no sailor he) always ended in a nightly truce and resulted in a lovely second honeymoon.

On the same visit I photographed the series of "Conor and Shelley" for Ladies' Home Journal *to illustrate an excerpt from* Trinity. *With a Dublin model and a Kerry friend we spent two days of heavenly exploration around Kerry's St. Finan's Bay. Other days we would drive the western peninsulas, always overwhelmed by the startling drama of Ireland's coast which seemed like a magnificently beautiful*

Connemara

woman but alas, cold and remote. Ireland's virgin beaches have been left unspoiled because of unfriendly chilling breezes and freezing water. Her sea commands respect and has punished those who have taken her lightly. There is a catalogue of shipwrecks from time immemorial, the most famous of which was a large part of the Spanish Armada.

The following year we returned to scout out locations for the motion picture of Trinity. Traveling with a director, producer and cinematographer we revisited our favorite places. Our imaginations soared as we filled the countryside with fictitious villages, characters, raids and romantic happenings. This particular trip was highlighted by the launching of the British editions of Ireland, A Terrible Beauty and Trinity which was celebrated at the legendary Abbey Theatre in Dublin.

Our most recent visit was for a very wet month of August. On assignment to photograph calendars, we covered thousands of miles in the West, especially the counties of Cork, Kerry and Galway. Our one sunny day came after four days of waiting to take a boat out to the Skellig Islands. The reward was worth the wait. The skipper maneuvered his boat into the treacherous swells of a cove of the Little Skellig where I could photograph the thousands of pairs of nesting gannets cramming every inch over every ledge. And later we watched these magnificent birds dive from the height of a hundred feet into the water after fish. The climax of the day was a tricky landing on the Great Skellig and a walk up six hundred feet of ancient steps carved into a cliffside to a monastery on the top. Legends? Why, Skellig Michael alone could provide enough for a night of banshee talk around a turf fire.

For the balance of this particular trip the weather was so fierce we nearly rusted, but don't you know that Guinness can oil your joints as well as your tongue.

And finally we discovered County Wicklow, perhaps the most beautiful in all of Ireland with her hidden valleys and scented woods still echoing the words of bygone patriots who hid there and of great scholarly monks who studied there. We were graced by the most generous hospitality on this latest visit and it merely served as an appetizer for the next revisit.

After each trip the headlines from the North became more piercing. The people in the Republic wish the "troubles" would just drift away. After all, they are finally building their own country and who needs the continuing hostility and fanaticism of Ulster? Yet, they are a proud people, proud of their wildness and sometimes pugnacious for the sake of being pugnacious. They may have been diluted but never broken; the British battering rams haven't pierced their armor of wit or their counteroffensive of words. But as British injustice continues the unwanted war in Ulster will also continue. President John Kennedy's words come to mind, "Those who make peaceful revolution impossible will make violent revolution inevitable."

Over the last ten years I have visited Ireland six times. I always arrive with anticipation, wanting to be haunted by her mysteries and teased by her fantasies. I traveled through her tortured landscape wondering what it is about this place that entices me so. Is it ancient ruins, wild seascapes, the hundred shades of green? Or is it the verbal jousting and continual singsong of stories in a language that is something beyond English…yet not quite foreign? It is all of these and more; it is a people whose goal is only to be themselves, whose spirit retains a dignity which is rare in today's world. It is the Irish refusal to be servants to anyone but their own minds.

JILL URIS

Man of Inishmaan, Aran Islands

St. Finan's Bay, County Kerry

Gweebarra Bay, County Donegal

Kerry

Mysterious, stunning Kerry. To tour the peninsulas of Kerry is to travel through centuries of habitation and over continents of scenery. MacGillycuddy's Reeks, the highest peaks in Ireland, hover over the moody lakes of Killarney while intimidating cliffs embrace lonely beaches. Breathtaking vistas hide behind the ever threatening mists.

Ring forts show settlement began around 1500 B.C. The multitudes of stone fences were built by every successive generation. History is recorded in sixth-century mortarless beehive huts, eighth-century Celtic high crosses, twelfth-century Romanesque round towers and fourteenth-century Norman keeps and castles as well as a famed Franciscan abbey.

Legends abound bringing the ruins to life. The fighting spirit of the Kerryman dates back to A.D. 200 when Finn MacCool, the legendary King of Ireland, fought a battle of a year and a day with Daire Domhain, "King of the World." Christianity was fortified in Kerry by St. Finan, the leper, who built the cliffside monastery on Skellig Michael Island in the sixth century. St. Brendan and a boatload of monks set out from Kerry some fourteen hundred years ago to discover the new world.

The glorious vistas of the Ring of Kerry are sobered by ghost houses that dot the landscape. Castle ruins stand as reminders of the Cromwellian Wars of the 1600s. Remnants of cottages tumbled by the battering rams of the British landlords or simply abandoned to the hunger of the potato famine of the last century are grim memorials to Ireland's agony of 1845–49 in which a million fell to disease and starvation and another million fled the country.

Bent but not broken, the Kerryman is a poet in a land of poets. Perhaps unlettered, but not unlearned, the Kerry peasant is a cunning storyteller who will charm you with his own version of Cathleen ni Houlihan, the ancient legend of Mother Ireland, then quickly sober you with a patriot's speech from the dock.

Valentia Island

A half-mile bridgehop from the mainland coast of Kerry, Valentia earned fame in the last century as the terminal for the first transatlantic cable. Today, she's a haven for deep-sea fishing and diving. One Kerry weather forecast goes, "If you look across the water and you can see Valentia Island then it is going to rain, but if you can't see the island then it is already raining."

Farmer, Iveragh Peninsula

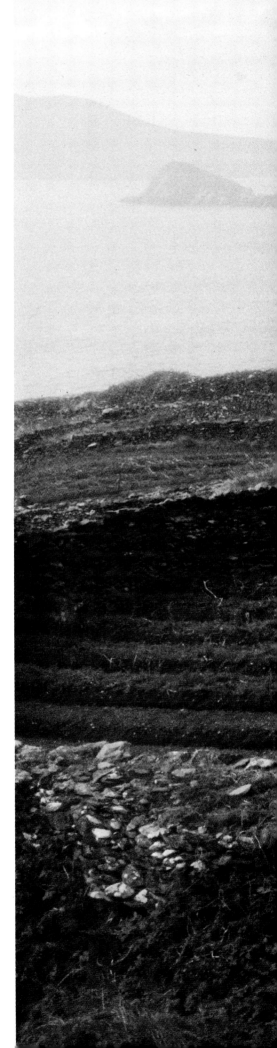

Slea Head, Dingle Peninsula

The rundale is an ancient system of land division culminating in thousands of postage-stamp-sized plots. The rocky land and buffeting Atlantic winds make the farmer's life no easy challenge.

"Some of the plots were hardly larger than our best room and very few people could really tell what exactly belonged to whom. Each plot was walled off, making a spider web of stone over the mountainside."

Leon Uris, *TRINITY*

HOG'S HEAD, RING OF KERRY

"The beautiful green country unfolded, a little melancholy for lack of light and shade,...for lack of a ray to gild the fields. A beautiful country falling into ruin."

George Moore, MOUNT VENUS

The farm is nestled between Ballinskelligs and the sweep of St. Finan's Bay at the Atlantic's edge of County Kerry. His house is modest and his land is poor but the life of this Kerryman is indeed rich in human values.

"They say that there may be a speck of quiet lodged at the central point of a cyclone. Round it everything goes whirling. It alone sits at its ease, as still as the end of an axle that lets the wheel, all about it, whirl any wild way it likes."

C. E. Montague,
ANOTHER TEMPLE GONE

"The grainy sand had gone from under his feet. His boots trod again a damp crackling mast, razorshells, squeaking pebbles, that on the unnumbered pebbles beats, wood sieved by the shipworm, lost Armada...farther away chalkscrawled backdoors and on the higher beach a dryingline with two crucified shirts."

James Joyce, ULYSSES

"Come away, O human child!
To the waters and the wild
With a faery, hand in hand,
For the world's more full of
     weeping than you
     can understand."

W. B. Yeats,
THE STOLEN CHILD

Calvary, Slea Head

The end of the Dingle Peninsula, the end of Ireland, the end of Europe; the next parish is Boston.

Shrine Near Waterville

"Turning and turning in the widening gyre The falcon cannot hear the falconer;...Surely some revelation is at hand; Surely the Second Coming is at hand....
And what rough beast, its hour come round at last, Slouches towards Bethlehem to be born?"

W. B. Yeats, THE SECOND COMING

SURF

"Listen: a fourworded wavespeech: seesoo, hrss, rsseeiss, ooos. Vehement breath of waters amid seasnakes, rearing horses, rocks. In cups of rocks it slops: flop, slop, slap: bounded in barrels. And spent, its speech ceases. It flows purling, widely flowing, floating foampool, flower unfurling."

James Joyce, ULYSSES

Evening Tide,
Rossbeigh Strand

Dirty Weather, Portmagee

A Rare Moment of Calm,
St. Finan's Bay

Boulder Beach and Remnants of Minard Castle
This ancient stronghold was shattered by Cromwellian troops in 1650;
Dingle Peninsula.

Sneem

Matt Courtney, Waterville

Chapel at Derrynane Abbey

DERRYNANE, HOME OF THE "LIBERATOR," DANIEL O'CONNELL

Kerry-born Daniel O'Connell was the people's hero of the last century. Affectionately called "King of the Beggars," he was committed to non-violence as he championed emancipation for the Catholics and repeal of the Union with England.

"When Dan spoke there was fearful trembling in the seats of the mighty. In him the nation that was dumb had found a voice. The despised had found a champion and the cruelly wronged an avenger. He was to them in the rank of the gods....His personal friend O'Niell Daunt...said of O'Connell, 'Well may his countrymen feel pride in the extraordinary man, who, for a series of years, could assail and defy a hostile and powerful government, who could knit together a prostrate, divided, and dispirited nation into a resolute and invincible confederacy; who could lead his followers in safety through the traps and pitfalls that beset their path to freedom; who could baffle all the artifices of sectarian bigotry; and finally overthrow the last strongholds of anti-Catholic tyranny by the simple might of public opinion.'"

Seumas MacManus, *THE STORY OF THE IRISH RACE*

The Lakes of Killarney

"I will arise and go now, and go to
    Innisfree,
And a small cabin build there, of
    clay and wattles made:
Nine bean-rows will I have there,
    a hive for the honeybee,
And live alone in the bee-loud
    glade.

And I shall have some peace there,
    for peace comes dropping slow,
Dropping from the veils of the
    morning to where the cricket
    sings;
There midnight's all a glimmer,
    and noon a purple glow,
And evening full of the linnet's
    wings.

I will arise and go now, for always
    night and day
I hear lake water lapping with low
    sounds by the shore;
While I stand on the roadway, or
    on the pavements grey,
I hear it in the deep heart's core."

W. B. Yeats, THE LAKE ISLE
    OF INNISFREE

FAIR DAY

Aye, the bargaining is fierce. After a bout of insulting theatrics a deal is made in the softest of whispers and confirmed with a blank nod. A mighty slap of the hand seals the transaction and it's off for a pint.

CONOR AND SHELLEY, A LOVE STORY

"In the days that followed her first meetings with Conor Larkin, Shelley found her placid existence upheaved. He was an entirely new sort of person, neither Shankill nor gentry. Actually, he fell into no category except his own....

It was those late parts of the evenings when the easiest rapport she had ever known with a man plunged them past midnight and time fleeted unaware. Shelley found herself intensely desiring to absorb his thoughts, but it was more...an unexplained outcropping of silliness that came on waves of sheer gaiety. She delighted when he was happy, for she sensed that laughter had not come easily and she discovered ways to make him laugh.

Then came that Sunday, and the night after the nights after that. She had not known a man could be so gentle, thoughtful and tender, yet so commanding. It was a moon trip from the beginning and it never came down....

Conor and Shelley counted the steps in unison as they climbed upward through the glen to a shimmering hazel grove a thousand feet over the lough....

Shelley lay back lovely on the grass, her red hair all floating in and out of deep green blades an the sun making her skin whiten to near translucence. Conor propped on an elbow and kissed her cheek and forehead and the tip of her nose and her eyes, 'Did I ever tell you how glad I am to have made your acquaintance, lady?'

'Oh, no, never,' she answered.

'Well, let me tell you then. I've walked through crowds of crowds all my life. I've seen the faces of the women in the church and heard the listless priest intone. I've seen the men come down from the fields and be felled to their knees at the angelus. I've seen the hard cities. And all the time I looked past sterile eyes into sterile hearts. Then one time I looked and it was different than all the·

other times and I told myself I'd have to be the worst kind of fool to recognize something had happened and not do something about it.'

Tears moistened in her eye. 'Of all the luck,' she whispered, 'finding myself a bard. You people have a way with words.'

'Aye, we're a canny and clever lot, for words are all we've had. But they're only your own thoughts coming back to you. You make me say things I no longer care to hide and I have no fear of hearing my own voice saying them.'

Shelley rolled away from him, sat and shook the grass from her hair and dress, then laid her cheek on her knees and hummed softly.

'Dusty Bluebells.'...

He put his hands beneath her arms and lifted her off her feet so they were eye to eye, with him holding her in mid-air. He wrapped her inside his arms and kissed her.

'I love you, lass,' he said, 'I love you.'...

The place was hauntingly devoid of life, leaving Shelley and Conor virtually alone on the long promenade with the sand and the sea and only the shrill cry of the gulls and the thump of the breakers....

What had begun in Belfast took wing, ethereal wing, in the gray brooding place. They were neither alive nor dead, but suspended, out in infinity, a vast timeless space. They realized at once that this journey could go on forever, they could explore it together and never need to retrace their steps, for what was always ahead was endless love-making, each time new, each time completely different. Perhaps they were doing much of the same thing over with their bodies but that was not how their minds read it.

They stood before a cave, its entrance blocked by a huge boulder which gave way. They entered together, for that was the only way in, in pairs. Eternities were opened as they knew they had come into the unique gift of constant and complete regeneration. A floating kind of thing that went on and on. It was awesome to comprehend that they had discovered nirvana....

Each night and during the days as well, they walked into the cave to fly and were shortly in a place of tens of trillions of galaxies, exploring in a web of miracle. When they knew they had reached the final nirvana, they found another even more thrilling...again and again...."

Leon Uris, TRINITY

GREAT BLASKET ISLAND

"On this sea-birds' ledge of Europe, where the Atlantic waves rise up like swallows into the lofts of air, a hardy community of people kept a bare foothold for centuries. It was a slackening hold when I saw it fifteen years ago, for the island was plainly exhausted and the girls from the mainland would no longer marry into it; only fifty people were left on it. The few green fields ringworming the rough hairy hillside, the old man holding on the tail of his donkey as it climbed the mountainy path, the old woman hunkered at her cottage door, her face sunk in her hands, the absence of children playing, gave the place an air of approaching dereliction. Yet this small island had been a crowded nest of Gaelic life and storytelling, and had contributed several minor classics to the world of books: THE ISLANDMAN, by Tomas O Crohan; TWENTY YEARS AGROWING, by Maurice O'Sullivan; and now Peig's own REFLECTIONS."

W. R. Rodgers' introduction to Peig Sayers'
AN OLD WOMAN'S REFLECTIONS

Lying three stormy miles off the Dingle Peninsula, the Blaskets were settled since medieval times. Great Blasket Island's population often doubled to accommodate starving peasants fleeing the mainland. In 1957 the little colony was beaten and the island abandoned.

Christ's Saddle, Skellig Michael

George Bernard Shaw described this island as having "The magic that takes you out, far out, of this time and this world."

SKELLIG ISLANDS

Two towering sea crags rising off the coast of Kerry are like mighty sailing ships defending the mainland. Skellig Michael houses a modern lighthouse as well as remnants of a well-preserved sixth-century monastic settlement, but is accessible by sea only on a rare calm summer day. The foreboding experience of climbing the ancient stairs carved into a steep cliffside past Stations of the Cross to the tiny beehive huts of the monastery rewards one with total exhilaration. Mere survival here by the ancient monks boggles the mind.

Her sister island, the Little Skellig, has known but a handful of human footsteps for the sea never slows its pounding long enough for a boat to land. Nonetheless a few brave souls have jumped ashore to observe the habits of the seabirds and seals who inhabit the rock. Twenty thousand pairs of nesting gannets make the Little Skellig the second largest gannet sanctuary in the world. The noble birds glide along the water then suddenly rise a hundred feet to plunge like kamikazes into the sea catching their dinner. Every accessible ledge of the island is fiercely defended as family territory where the takeoffs and landings are controlled as if by direction of a sophisticated airport tower.

Way of the Cross, Skellig Michael

Known as the Wailing Woman, this stone is reputed to be one of the Stations of the Cross visited by pilgrims from the Middle Ages through the last century.

Beehive Huts of the Ancient Monastery, Skellig Michael

Des Lavelle, Boatman, Naturalist and Author

Son, grandson and great-grandson of lighthouse keepers, Des Lavelle lives on Valentia Island and travels to the Skelligs every chance he has. His book *Skellig, Island Outpost of Europe,* is a little masterpiece covering the history, geology, bird and plant life on the islands.

Christ's Saddle, Skellig Michael

Gannets, Little Skellig

"The 'Changing of the Guard' at the nest when the gannet returns from a fishing trip is a highly ceremonious show – ...

Both birds stand face to face, wings half open, bowing to each other and knocking their bills together with much contented grunting. No doubt it could be a very graceful affair if they had enough space, but in the crowded conditions of the Small Skellig, any protruding wingtip or tail which encroaches by an inch on a neighbour's territory is liable to provoke a sharp stab of retaliation which upsets the whole ceremony."

Des Lavelle, *SKELLIG, ISLAND OUTPOST OF EUROPE*

Cork

One feels the skies weeping over Cork Harbor, in despair for the scene of those thousands of émigrés departing their homeland forever. Today, however, many are coming home, business is booming and Cork has again become a young people's city. Settled gently along the River Lee, friendly Cork boasts an impressive and varied list of famous sons: fierce fighters for Irish independence Tom Barry and Michael Collins; the assassinated Lord Mayor Tomas MacCurtain and his successor, the martyr Terence MacSwiney, who died after seventy-four days on hunger strike in the English Brixton Prison in 1920. His words became an inspiration for future Irish martyrs: "It is not those who can inflict the most, but those that can suffer the most who will conquer."

As a cultural center Cork has been home to a number of fine writers and artists: Frank O'Connor, Sean O Faolain and Daniel Corkery are masters of fiction, while Seamus Murphy and Marshall Hutson are among Ireland's greatest artists.

Tattered Grace, Cork City

Lace Curtain Colleen
No matter where the Irish wandered or how poorly their fate, the lace curtain traveled as the one symbol of the elegance that is their charm.

"*Slowly waking up, dreaming, storing up scenes and memories from zeppelins to basking sharks, traveling without moving, always imagining and remembering people and times.*"
Marshall Hutson, Sunday's Well, Cork

Passersby

Gougane Barra, County Cork

"You'll hear sounds you never heard before. These sounds will come from the wood. There is music in the pine that is in no other tree, faint and melancholy music that the tree gives forth as if it were ever lamenting the dead. Should there be a strong wind you will hear a wonderful noise on the tops of the bare branches—the ghosts and evil spirits of the woods fighting out their battles in the darkness of the night. But if the night be calm you will hear other music overhead, a soft lullaby that would put even a murderer to sleep."

Patráic Ó Conaire, FIELD AND FAIR

Manor House, Mallow

The Protestant ascendancy continues to live a separate life. Yesterday's London *Evening News* is delivered in the morning post. A huge portrait of William of Orange, the seventeenth-century Protestant English monarch, dominates the dining room as afternoon tea is served at four with proper doilies.

Coulagh Bay, West Cork

THE WILD BERE PENINSULA, WEST CORK

Silvery mist carries the scent of the sea into sturdy houses tucked
among the boulders. The glory days of the copper mines are gone but
fuchsia-laden hedges and glacial formations along the coast lure
visitors in search of remote peace.

*"Small quilts of farms lost heart in their struggle against obdurate, peaty,
rocky earth and disappeared altogether. Then there was nothing but barren bog-
land and here and there an occasional gnarled tree, its back to the ocean, its
tortuous arms outstretched to the shelter of the interior."*

Brian Friel, THE SAUCER OF THE LARKS

Friends, Allihies, West Cork

Monday Morning, Public House, Allihies, West Cork

Remnants of Dunboy Castle, Castletownbere, West Cork

*"In all the rooms, all the cheap crockery stood quiet on the shelves; the chairs
leaned against the shaky walls; rosy-faced fires had all gone pale; the patter
of children's feet had long since ceased; only dreams crept slyly in to fill the ugly
rooms with sparkling peace for a few dark moments, clothing the sleepers with a
cautious splendour; setting them, maybe, to sip rare wines from bulging bottles,
or led them to yellow sands bordering a playful sea. A younger lass, perhaps,
dreamed of scanty night attire between snowy sheets, with a colour-robed prince by
the bedroom door in haste to come in, and bid her a choice goodnight; while the
younger men saw themselves, sword in hand, driving the khaki cut-throats out of
Eire's five beautiful fields."*

Sean O'Casey, THE RAID

Bere Haven

*"All around the south coast inlets, accepted as part of the landscape are the stark,
almost surrealistic bones of old ships. Dreamlike memories of long ago. On grey
days of rain and mist they conjour up fancies of a ship wreck accident or sudden
calamity. Up beyond Belgooly and down to Glandore one sees them, half sunken
in the mud of tidal creeks, their blackened bones festooned with funereal seaweed."*

Marshall Hutson, a private correspondence, Sunday's Well, Cork

Clare

CLIFFS OF MOHER, COUNTY CLARE

"Rampart after rampart of uncompromising cliffside sliced jaggedly down, down, down; the troubled sea is so far below that its cliff-foot brawl is but a rumour of remote battle carried upwards on a fitful wind. This indeed is Moher."

Bryan MacMahon, HERE'S IRELAND

O'Brien's Tower, Cliffs of Moher

Lahinch on Liscannor Bay, County Clare

Galway

CONNEMARA

"For the strangers came and tried to teach us their way
They scorned us just for being what we are
But they might as well go chasing after moonbeams
Or light a penny candle from a star."

GALWAY BAY

A rugged lunarscape where secret lakes, craggy bens and eternal rock blend in a sad beauty; where bits of color struggle through waves of granite fields; where vibrations of the "other world" invade the imagination. Sure there's a lair of "little people" between the hedge and the river bend. Remember stories of famine days when the villagers survived on nettles and cabbage leaves. In one village three hundred people were forced out of their homes to sleep in holes dug in the earth roofed over with sticks and turf like a pheasant's nest.

This is the land of the Gaeltacht, where keepers of the ancient ways are forever struggling to only be themselves, and where Gaelic is still the spoken word.

The Connemara folk are proud survivors of a cruel land where rocks and death are facts of life. The tractor isn't used much in these parts where a man alone can better dig up the rocks, build the walls and harvest the tiny plots. Gnarled, wild, turbulent faces match the landscape, but a strong spirit pervades with values beyond comfort as fortification. The sweet smell of the peat fire lures one into a wee cottage where there's always an extra potato and a hunk of soda bread for the stranger. A dresser displays the family heirlooms, dishes and teacups with a blue willow pattern. The picture on the wall is of the Holy Family, Mary dressed in blue with a red mantle and an Irish-looking Jesus in bare feet.

Under the Twelve Bens

"Little fields with boulders dotted,
Grey-stone shoulders saffron-spotted,
Stone-walled cabins thatched with reeds,
Where a Stone Age people breeds
*   The last of Europe's stone age race."*

John Betjeman, SUNDAY IN IRELAND

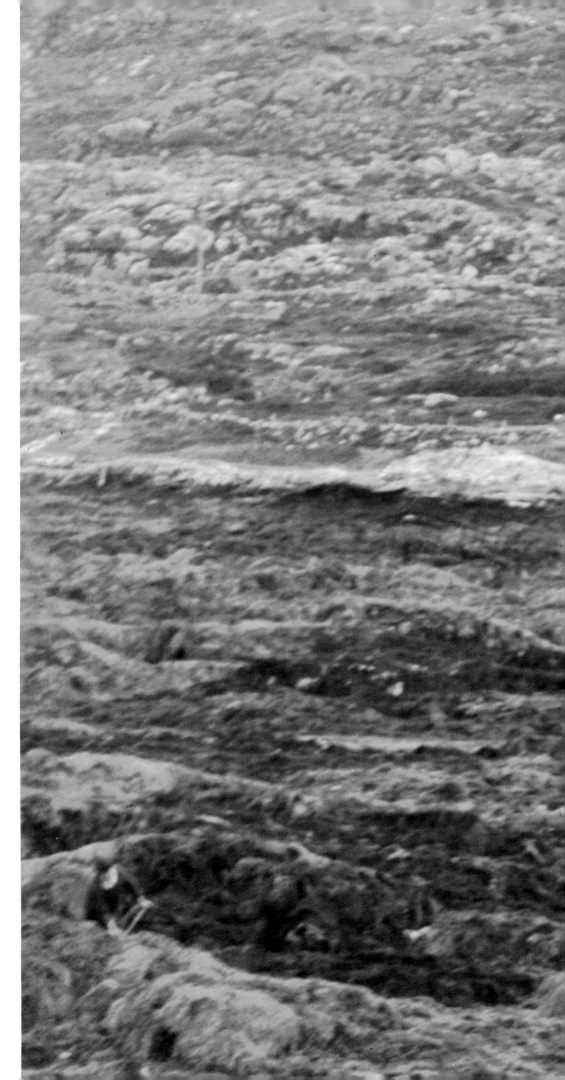

Gathering Seaweed

"Daddo told us that before the famine the seaweed harvesters would work naked, which was both practical and comfortable. However, the good priests took over blessing this enterprise and naturally we had to preserve our morals, so the only thing bare any more was our feet....

Part of the wrack rights included taking shellfish. Throughout the night, parties of boys and girls dug for clams and scallops and oysters and chipped mussels off the rocks. This was the part Conor and I liked best because we'd choose our girls weeks in advance....

Separating the kelp was a great and messy chore. Some of it was used for animal fodder, some for making iodine and some for fertilizer. There was edible seaweed that my ma mixed with potatoes and another type that could be jellied to thicken the milk and butter.

Oily fires smoked along the coast to burn the weed down and boil it for use in making soap and bleach, and yet other kelp was watered down to preserve the shellfish. Shells were crushed and made into whitewash. A few weeks after the wracking was done our cottages gleamed with new coats."

Leon Uris, TRINITY

Binding the Stalks

Carraroe

In 1880 a young man of this village took a wife without prior consent of his landlord and his rent was raised as punishment. Rent raisings and evictions were commonplace, the harvest was poor and the villagers massed in anger. Thus began the battle of the tenants which led to the aid of the Land League which fought for tenants' rights in the courts in Dublin and London.

The sister of Charles Stewart Parnell, champion of the Land League, wrote these verses:

"The serpent's curse upon you lies—ye writhe within the dust,
Ye fill your mouths with beggars' swill, ye grovel for a crust;
Your lords have set their blood-stained heels upon your shameful heads,
Yet they are kind—they leave you still their ditches for your beds!"

Miss Fanny Parnell

Roadside Shrine, Connemara

"Working all my life I am, working with the flail in the barn, working with a spade at the potato tilling and the potato digging, breaking stones on the road, and four years ago the wife died, and it's lonesome to be in the house keeping alone."

Lady Gregory, *THE KILTARTAN BOOKS*

Roundstone Charmer

"If cows could eat [the rocks] this place would make a grand dairy farm....You ought to pay me, instead, for occupying this rockpile, miscalled a farm. But I have fine reports to give you of a promising harvest. The milkweed and thistles is in thriving condition, and I never saw the poison ivy so bounteous and beautiful."

Eugene O'Neill, *A MOON FOR THE MISBEGOTTEN*

PREVIOUS PAGES:

Kylemore Abbey

Built in the middle of the last century by an English surgeon, this granite fortress was the epitome of luxury featuring a royal ballroom, oak balustrades, stained-glass windows and beveled mirrors. Gutted by fire in 1959, the mansion is today a Benedictine abbey. When the lake is calm one might chance a peek at the nuns fishing.

Ballynahinch Lake

Guarded by a dozen bald mountains, hunting lodges, riding trails, castles and abbeys are tucked in bends of the river.

ASHFORD CASTLE, CONG

Remains of a twelfth-century Augustinian abbey founded by the last high king of Ireland, Rory O'Connor, and his grave stand guard over this delightful village on the Galway-Mayo border. In more recent history Cong gained fame as the locale of the film *The Quiet Man*.

Set on the shores of Lough Corrib, the fairly-tale mansion of Ashford Castle includes remains of a thirteenth-century castle and remnants of a French château. The castle underwent considerable renovation in the nineteenth century under the ownership of the famed Guinness family. Now a superbly appointed hotel owned by the Mulcahy family, the castle grounds include a top-notch golf course, fine fishing streams and hunting grounds, making the area a haven for sportsmen.

Cornamona, County Galway

Cong River

"But now they drift on the still water,
Mysterious, beautiful;
Among what rushes will they build,
By what lake's edge or pool
Delight men's eyes when I awake some day
To find they have flown away?"

W. B. Yeats, THE WILD SWANS AT COOLE

Barge on the Shannon

Along the River Shannon

"Now it's July, hot and sleepy and still;
The noontide hanging motionless over the hill
Like a pike in a pool. And the glossy flies
Are flashing like great sun-whips across the eyes."

W. R. Rodgers, SUMMER JOURNEY

Donegal

Moving north and away from the raging western coast, the land turns rolling and gentler. Bright yellow beaches, dunes, fjords, coves and caves wend from Killybegs to Bloody Foreland to Lough Foyle. County Donegal gives an insatiable feeling of romantic remoteness, where whispering grasses blend in a pastoral of greens.

"For what good is a bit of a farm with cows on it, and sheep on the back hills, when you do be sitting looking out from a door the like of that door, and seeing nothing but the mists rolling down the bog, and the mists again and they rolling up the bog, and hearing nothing but the wind crying out in the bits of broken trees were left from the great storm, and the streams roaring with the rain."

J. M. Synge, *IN THE SHADOW OF THE GLEN*

Tawny Bay

Bachelor Brothers, Carrigart

They invited us in out of the rain to a cottage which had scarcely seen change in 150 years. A peat fire was going under the caldron of potatoes; a single ten-watt light bulb was the sole show of change and affluence.

"Ye see," he explained, "the problem was that the land was divided into three halves. Our half was always the worst of the lot."

Brian Friel's Beach Near Bloody Foreland

"Dammit, it's lovely, isn't it, eh? God Himself above you and the best of creation all round you....I wouldn't mind being laid to rest anywhere along the coast here myself...it would be nice to have the sea near you and the birds above you wouldn't it?...Out here, man, you still have life all around you. Dammit, there's so much good life all around you, you haven't a chance to be really dead!"

Brian Friel, THE SAUCER OF THE LARKS

Killybegs

The herring has been caught, gutted and taken off to the morning market. The midday pier is full of lonely sounds. Listen now to the groan of the trawlers and the twang of their lines; the squawks of the greedy gulls and the bluster of their wings; the creaking wood of the pier and the slow splash of the waves.

Derry

LONDONDERRY AIR

Nowhere is the colonization of Ireland more repugnant and volatile than in the city which bears the name of the Guild of London merchants. From the old wall built in 1618 two youngsters look down on the Bogside. From here arrogant Protestant Orangemen annually taunted the native Catholic "croppies" by raining pennies down on them.

In 1689, thirty thousand Protestants led by thirteen apprentice boys, locked themselves inside the city's gates as defense against Catholic forces of King James II. The siege lasted 105 days; however, siege mentality continues to hover over Derry's daily life where the Catholic population is still ghettoized in the lowlands and outskirts of the city. Protestants make up only a third of the population but they have the better jobs, housing and education. Injustice has brought on protest which grew into terrorism that has slowly destroyed most of the inner city.

House Painter, Derry

Derry

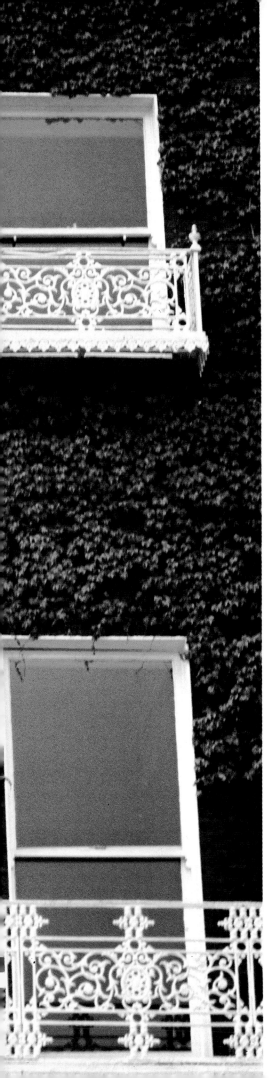

Dublin

Dublin is a city like no other city. Her grandeur is different than the grandeur of other places which shout it out in marble palaces and sky-scrapers. Dublin has few of these. The public buildings of the nation's capital are handsome but hardly impressive. She is a bit shabby for the land she rules is poor; however, her precious elegance shines like the tattered threads of an aged grande dame who holds her head high with dignity.

What Dublin has is a uniqueness built from language. Language of those playing the patriot's game, language of poets and playwrights and language of just plain talk. Speeches from the dock, speeches from the graveside, speeches from the stage and a torrent of printed words bespeak the national longing that has designated Dublin as a different and special place in all the world. Her dim cobblestone streets, her var-nished pubs, her vaunted stages, her genteel drawing rooms and abys-mal slums are yet haunted by the grief and anger of defiant sons and daughters whose words have become the gospel of nationhood.

It is an overwhelmingly Catholic city in numbers but the Georgian row houses and petit squares recall an Anglo-Irish ascendancy many of whom were no less Irish than their Catholic brothers. Jonathan Swift, Oliver Goldsmith, George Bernard Shaw and William Butler Yeats are among her immortal Protestant writers. Two of her earliest republican martyrs were Protestant as well. Theobald Wolfe Tone, son of a Dublin coachmaker, leads the roll call of heroes who gave their lives for Irish freedom. He was the first of the great rebels to try to unite the nation and was put to death for his aborted Uprising of 1798. And Wolfe Tone was followed by Robert Emmet, son of a Dublin physician, who in 1803 led another disastrous rebellion. But what lived beyond Emmet were his immortal words spoken from the dock before his execution at Kilmain-ham Jail, which became the future generations' battle cry for freedom:

"When my country takes her place among the nations of the earth, then and not till then, let my epitaph be written."

At the beginning of the twentieth century Dublin, which had long been the seat of the loathed English power, became the wellspring of a great Irish renaissance. The majesty and rage of words in English and in Gaelic exploded like a mushroom cloud. To augment the literary revival a Gaelic League came into being to promote all those things which were uniquely Irish from Gaelic football and hurling to the old language, inspiring young men and women to remember their ancient Gaelic glory.

In the ivy-covered Georgian townhouses along Merrion Square and St. Stephen's Green activists and politicians gathered and planned. Charles Stewart Parnell became the first to organize the Irish people into a united front, taking scores of Irishmen into the British House of Commons to join the battle through political action. And later a new and more rebellious direction was found with the birth of the political party Sinn Fein, which means "Ourselves Alone." And with the political arm came the military arm, the Irish Republican Army.

Dublin's renaissance was highlighted by a number of uncommon women. There was Maud Gonne, a six-foot beauty who became Ire-land's most famous actress. She was the inspiration yet unrequited love of poet W. B. Yeats. A feminist decades ahead of her time, she stalked

Merrion Square

Dublin Castle

Site of the seat of British power in Ireland for nearly five hundred years. Today the elegant apartments are used for state occasions.

the land for reform, bore a daughter out of wedlock with a French activist and eventually married an Irish soldier of fortune, John MacBride, who died before a British firing squad. Their son, Sean MacBride, won the Nobel Peace Prize in 1974 for his work as a founder of Amnesty International.

And there was the aristocrat Countess Constance Markievicz, who led the suffragette movement and later became a commander of the Irish Republic Army and served as a defiant guest in a score of British prisons.

Many of the Irish aspirations were crystallized by yet another woman, Lady Gregory, who gathered and wrote many of Ireland's legends as they had been told around the turf fires by country bards. She with Yeats founded the Abbey Theatre, where the tenements of O'Casey, the cottages of Synge and the pubs and back streets of Joyce came to life on stage.

By 1915 Dublin was sizzling with patriotic fever in search of a martyr. The role was filled by an old warrior of the failed Fenian Rising of 1867 who had lived in exile in America. After his death Jeremiah O'Donovan Rossa was returned to Dublin for burial. His funeral erupted the pent-up emotions of the people with a cortege that numbered in the hundreds of thousands. Words spoken over his grave by the patriot-poet Padraic Pearse were of the stuff to fan the flames of smoldering republicanism:

"…we pledge to Ireland our love, and we pledge to English rule in Ireland our hate…life springs from death: and from the graves of patriot men and women spring living nations…the Defenders of this realm…think they have pacified Ireland…the fools, the fools, the fools! They have left us our Fenian dead, and while Ireland holds these graves, Ireland unfree shall never be at peace."

The moment of reckoning came on Easter Monday in 1916 when Dublin hosted the opening battle for Irish freedom. Her declaration of independence is yet another example of Ireland's most powerful weapon, language.

"Irishmen and Irishwomen: In the name of God and of the dead generations from which she receives her old tradition of nationhood, Ireland, through us, summons her children to her flag and strikes for her freedom....We declare the right of the people of Ireland to the ownership of Ireland."

The Easter Rising itself was a short, bitter tragedy. But the British, who had scarcely learned a thing in seven hundred years of dealing with these people, took the leaders of the rebellion out and shot them. This act created sixteen martyrs, and aroused the people to join the battle for eventual nationhood.

Dublin is not only the city of revolutionaries and writers, she is the city of individuals who glory in talk. Every man and woman has a unique style of expression where each word is selected with care, weaving ornate tapestries of conversation. Ordinary city noises are drowned out by the chat and laughter as the day's work is postponed for the lilting sound of talk; talk of sports, weather, horses, cars, politics, gossip, you name it.

The gathering places are the churches, pubs and the sports park. But no matter what the occasion listen to the melodies, they're often more memorable than the substance. Dubliners pay little heed to fancy dress or the ordinary status symbols of affluence, however, a good listener or a fine conversationalist is always admired.

Dublin, the capital of a small but potent democracy? Well, yes, but modest in those pretensions. What is rich and what is value is that undeniable literary talent of an entire city; where every taxi driver and shopkeeper cherishes his own greatest treasure, his individual way with language.

The Markets

And your man said, "Go down and get your nose educated at the fish and vegetable markets."

St. Stephen's Green

"But the trees in Stephen's Green were fragrant of sea rain and the rain-sodden earth gave forth its mortal odour, a faint incense rising upward through the mould from many hearts."

James Joyce, A PORTRAIT OF THE ARTIST AS A YOUNG MAN

Joyce's View, Dun Laoghaire

"Woodshadows floating silently by through the morning peace from the stairhead seaward where he gazed. Inshore and farther out the mirror of water whitened, spurned by lightshod hurrying feet. White breast of the dim sea. The twining stresses, two by two."

James Joyce, ULYSSES

County Kildare

On the wooded grounds of Carton House in the heart of horse-breeding country a high-spirited thoroughbred represents a long-standing tradition.

Dublin Horse Show, Ballsbridge

The Royal Dublin Society, founded in 1731, sponsors the week-long annual horse show drawing tens of thousands of visitors from all over Europe.

Day at the Races

In order to beat the sunset and the incoming tide the Laytown Races in County Meath are perhaps the only festive occasion in Ireland to start on time.

"It's there you'll see thė gamblers, the thimbles and the garters, And the sporting
Wheel of Fortune with the four and twenty quarters."

Anonymous, GALWAY RACES

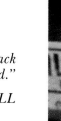

"You might as well try to catch a falling leaf as try to find out what's at the back
of Lally's mind."

Mary Lavin, THE WILL

Wicklow

"The Garden of Ireland."
Over round mountains,
through the heather, in and
out of wooded valleys, a
glimpse of the Irish Sea. The
glacial rocks, quiet lakes and
gentle mountains have pro-
vided refuge for saints and
chieftains. St. Kevin, the her-
mit, sought solitude at Glendalough where it is said he slept
in the hollow of a tree, and in
his later years established the
monastery which flourished
from the sixth through the sixteenth century.

In the sixteenth and seven-
teenth centuries the hills acted
as an impenetrable stronghold
of the O'Toole and O'Byrne
clans, who pestered the
English in Dublin with sudden
raids and cattle forays.

Today the Wicklow Moun-
tains are a refuge for city folk
and young people who crave a
moment's peace or a vigorous
afternoon's hunt with the
hounds either on a two-
wheeler or on a stately mare.

"The web the spider weaves
Is a glittering net;
The woodland path is wet,
And the soaking earth smells sweet,
Under my two bare feet
And the rain drips,
Drips, drips, drips from the leaves."

Winifred M. Letts, A SOFT DAY

GLENDALOUGH

This monastic city was founded by St. Kevin in the sixth century at a time when Ireland was the light of Western civilization. Monks and scholars studied and illuminated magnificent manuscripts and served as missionaries to pagan Britain and a dark European continent.

"With my heart full of joy I struck out through the Vale of Glendalough.... There lay the two silvery lakes encircled by lofty moonlit mountain peaks; there stood the old churches and the round tower in the distance resembling a vision one might see in a dream....I gazed across the lake at the spot where St. Kevin made his bed; he must have been a poet, a great poet, who selected such an abode....

Had I met an old pagan, or abbot, or saint from the past, I should not have been surprised; were they not all around me, had I but eyes to see them? Was I myself not like one enchanted, who, having thrown off the worries and anxieties of this world, was proceeding through a delightful old world from which had been cast out all evil and malice?"

Pátraic Ó Conaire, FIELD AND FAIR

"In the peerless panorama of Ireland's portfolio...of bosky grove and undulating plain and luscious pastureland of vernal green, steeped in the transcendent translucent glow of our mild mysterious Irish twilight..."

James Joyce, ULYSSES

Clanmore Castle, County Wicklow

"It was an afternoon in May—oh, fifteen years ago...the boat was blue and the paint was peeling and there was an empty cigarette packet floating in the water...between us at that moment there was this great happiness, this great joy...although nothing was being said—just the two of us fishing on a lake on a showery day—and young as I was I felt, I know, that this was precious, and your hat was soft on the top of my ears—I can feel it—and I shrank down into your coat—and then, then for no reason at all except that you were happy too, you began to sing....

Listen! Listen! Listen! Do you hear it? D'you know what the music says? It says that once upon a time a boy and his father sat in a blue boat on a lake on an afternoon in May, and on that afternoon a great beauty happened, a beauty that has haunted the boy ever since, because he wonders now did it really take place or did he imagine it. There are only the two of us, he says; each of us is all the other has; and why can we not even look at each other?"

Brian Friel, PHILADELPHIA, HERE I COME

The Beach at Wicklow Town

"All those holes and pebbles. Who could count them? Never know what you find. Bottle with story of a treasure in it thrown from a wreck. Parcels post. Children always want to throw things in the sea. Trust? Bread cast on the waters. What's this? Bit of stick."

James Joyce, ULYSSES

Kevin Windsor, Wicklow Farmer

Weekend Squire and His Lady

Weary of the Dublin dealing and dandy dress, they head for the hills on Friday. Into the Wellington boots, hair let down, she's a fine farmer with a good-sized vegetable patch and a greenhouse filled with flowers. If ever the sky lifts, it's off on the horses to the hunt. He'll tinker with his guns and bikes between visits with the neighbors laced with a drop of Paddy and plenty of conversation.

"Oh, then tell me, Sean O'Farrell,
   where the gathering is to be?
In the old spot by the river,
   right well known to you and me;
One more word for signal token,
   whistle up the marchin' tune,
With your pike upon your shoulder,
   by the risin' of the moon."

THE RISING OF THE MOON

Aran Islands

"There is no present or future, only the past happening over and over again, now."
Eugene O'Neill, A MOON FOR THE MISBEGOTTEN

ETERNAL IRELAND

They are the past. They are the banshees alone in the wind clinging and remembering. They have seen battle and famine and a billion tears of emigrants passing from Ireland's shores. They are what's left of a way of life and want no part of today or tomorrow and who's to say they're wrong? A beautiful defiance.

Dun Aengus

Hovering three hundred feet over Galway Bay, this prehistoric fort with walls up to eighteen feet thick and twenty feet high dominates the skyline of Inishmore. The three limestone slabs that form the Aran Islands of Inishmore, Inishmaan and Inisheer support a population of thirteen hundred souls clinging tenaciously to their own ways. History and legend join the wind and the sea as constant companions to the islanders. Ruins of forts, Christian monasteries and medieval castles give testimony to legends of ancient settlement. Inishmore was a learning center and retreat for early Christians from Europe just as today Inisheer is a learning center for Gaelic students. An Aran saying, "Solitude without loneliness" lures a number of visitors to the islands to listen to the purest Gaelic spoken and to see, hear and smell the sea mists roll over the islands as a protective shield from the madness of the outside world.

"Like a blessed barrier reef protecting holy Ireland, they stand up from the sea, defiant in their isolation, proud even in their uniqueness. If they are anything, they are isolated and unique. Scholars the world over, like pilgrims, trek to Aran to rub the limestone of a windswept geology, to search the mounds of Iron Age burials, to imagine a history that has not been recorded, to listen, finally, to the waves and the soft voices speaking in a nearly forgotten language."

Dennis Smith, ARAN ISLANDS, A PERSONAL JOURNEY

"*A week of sweeping fogs has passed over and given me a strange sense of exile and desolation. I walk round the island nearly every day, yet I can see nothing anywhere but a mass of wet rock, a strip of surf, and then a tumult of waves. The slaty limestone has grown black with the water that is dripping on it, and wherever I turn there is the same grey obsession twining and wreathing itself among the narrow fields, and the same wail from the wind that shrieks and whistles in the loose rubble of the walls.*"

J. M. Synge, THE ARAN ISLANDS

"*We are poor, simple people, living from hand to mouth. I fancy we should have been no better off if we had been misers. We were apt and willing to live, without repining, the life the Blessed Master made for us, often and again ploughing the sea with only our hope in God to bring us through. We had characters of our own, each different from the other, and all different from the landsmen; and we had our own little failings, too....*

This is a crag in the midst of the great sea, and again and again the blown surf drives right over it before the violence of the wind, so that you daren't put your head out any more than a rabbit that crouches in his burrow in Inishvickillaun when the rain and the salt spume are flying. Often would we put to sea at the dawn of day when the weather was decent enough, and by the day's end our people on land would be keening us, so much had the weather changed for the worse. It was our business to be out in the night, and the misery of that sort of fishing is beyond telling."

Tomas O Crohan, THE ISLANDMAN